Let's Explore
Math

by Joe Levit

LERNER PUBLICATIONS ◆ MINNEAPOLIS

Note to Educators:

Throughout this book, you'll find critical-thinking questions. These can be used to engage young readers in thinking critically about the topic and in using the text and photos to do so.

Lerner Publications Company
A division of Lerner Publishing Group, Inc.
241 First Avenue North
Minneapolis, MN 55401 USA

For reading levels and more information, look up this title at www.lernerbooks.com.

Library of Congress Cataloging-in-Publication Data

Names: Levit, Joseph, author.
Title: Let's explore math / by Joe Levit.
Other titles: Let us explore math
Description: Minneapolis : Lerner Publications, [2018] | Series: Bumba books. A first look at STEM | Audience: Ages 4-7. | Audience: K to grade 3. | Includes bibliographical references and index.
Identifiers: LCCN 2017058205 (print) | LCCN 2018002434 (ebook) | ISBN 9781541507821 (eb pdf) | ISBN 9781541503281 (lb : alk. paper) | ISBN 9781541527003 (pb : alk. paper)
Subjects: LCSH: Mathematics—Juvenile literature. | Measurement—Juvenile literature.
Classification: LCC QA113 (ebook) | LCC QA113 .L4784 2018 (print) | DDC 510—dc23

LC record available at https://lccn.loc.gov/2017058205

Manufactured in the United States of America
1-43823-33656-1/11/2018

Table of Contents

What Is Math? 4

Math Tools 22

Picture Glossary 23

Read More 24

Index 24

What Is Math?

Math means "the science

of numbers."

People use math to do

jobs or figure things out.

Math helps people plan a trip.

They think about how far they are going.

They figure out how many minutes it will take.

We use math to plan our day.

Math can tell us how long we

can play before it is time to eat.

How else can
math help
people make
plans?

Math helps us at the grocery store.

Food at the store has different prices.

People use math to compare the prices.

Math helps to bake a cake.

Count the eggs that will go

in the cake.

Use a tablespoon to

measure sugar.

What else can you make using math?

Work in a garden using math.

How far apart should the plants be?

Use a ruler to measure the distance.

15

Sometimes people use

computers to do math.

Computers can solve

problems quickly.

Math helps us learn about outer space. Scientists use math to study planets and stars.

You can use math

every day.

Think about a job you

must do.

Then use math to

help do it!

Math Tools

tablespoon

computer

clock

ruler

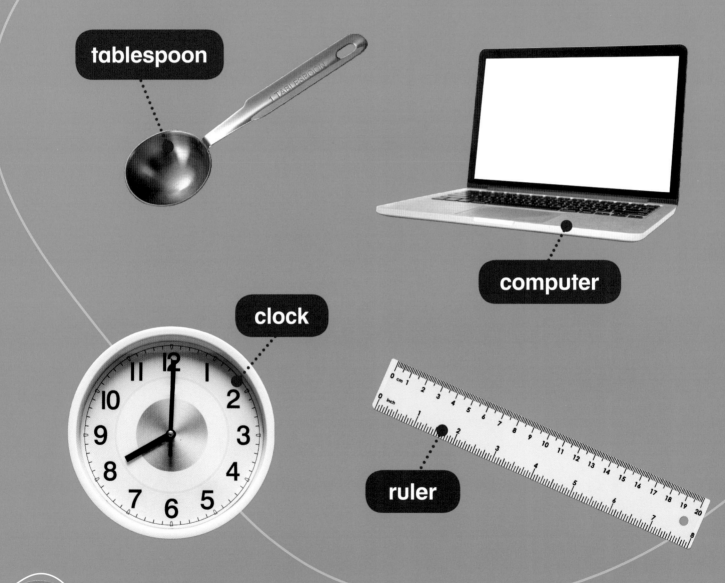

Picture Glossary

compare

see if two things
are alike or different

problems

questions

scientists

people who
study the world

tablespoon

a large spoon
used for measuring

23

Read More

Cleary, Brian P. *A Second, a Minute, a Week with Days in It: A Book about Time*. Minneapolis: Millbrook Press, 2013.

Rose, Deborah Lee. *The Twelve Days of Kindergarten: A Counting Book*. New York: Abrams Books for Young Readers, 2017.

Schuh, Mari. *The Crayola Counting Book*. Minneapolis: Lerner Publications, 2018.

Index

computer, 16

garden, 14

grocery store, 10

problem, 16

ruler, 14

tablespoon, 12

Photo Credits

The images in this book are used with the permission of: © Amy Salveson/Independent Picture Service (calculator design element); Phil's Mommy/Shutterstock.com, p. 5; LightField Studios/Shutterstock.com, p. 7; Africa Studio/Shutterstock.com, pp. 9, 15, 17; Syda Productions/Shutterstock.com, p. 11; Emotions studio/Shutterstock.com, pp. 12–13; frantic00/Shutterstock.com, p. 19; wavebreakmedia/Shutterstock.com, pp. 20–21; Afonkin_Y/Shutterstock.com, p. 22 (top left); Goran Bogicevic/Shutterstock.com, p. 22 (top right); Stas Knop/Shutterstock.com, p. 22 (bottom left); Ivsanmas/Shutterstock.com, p. 22 (bottom right); KK Tan/Shutterstock.com, p. 23 (top left); sakkmesterke/Shutterstock.com, p. 23 (top right); ProStockStudio/Shutterstock.com, p. 23 (bottom left); Tyler Olson/Shutterstock.com, p. 23 (bottom right).

Front cover: Thomas M Perkins/Shutterstock.com.